REA
PROCRASTINATE!

*23 Anti-Procrastination Tools Designed
to Help You Stop Putting Things Off
and Start Getting Things Done – Today!*

Akash P. Karia
#1 Amazon Bestselling Author Of
"How To Deliver A Great Ted Talk" and
"How To Design Ted-Worthy Presentation Slides"
www.AkashKaria.com

BESTSELLING BOOKS BY AKASH KARIA

Available on Amazon (www.bit.ly/AkashKaria):

How to Deliver a Great TED Talk

How to Design TED-Worthy Presentation Slides

Own the Room: Presentation Techniques to Keep Your Audience on the Edge of Their Seats

How Successful People Think Differently

ANTI Negativity: How to Stop Negative Thinking and Lead a Positive Life

Persuasion Psychology: 26 Powerful Techniques to Persuade Anyone!

FREE RESOURCES

There are hundreds of free articles as well as several eBooks, MP3s and videos on Akash's blog. To get instant access to those, head over to www.AkashKaria.com.

Copyright © 2015 Akash Karia
All rights reserved.
ISBN-13: 978-1507530320
ISBN-10: 1507530323

RAVE REVIEWS FOR "READY, SET... PROCRASTINATE"

"**This is one book you should not delay reading**! Having struggled with procrastination for much of my life, Akash Karia's book came like a breath of fresh air. He provides clear, practical advice on how to overcome the problem, but warns that you will need to work at it daily. This is a quick, very useful read and with 23 tips on offer, there will be several that you can identify with and implement for immediate results. If there is just one thing that you should not put off, it is reading this book."
~ Gillian Findlay

"**Great book**. There were many great ideas to try and implement to stop procrastinating. And it was a very easy and quick read."
~ LeAndria Corbett

"Useful and interesting. Interesting collections of tips. I could apply some of them "of the shelf". Just don't try to use them all, and don't expect that they will do your work. You still need to work hard, but you definitely have help in this book. **Go back from time to time to it, see if you see it in a different light**."
~ Dan Luca

"I am one of the biggest procrastinators so I had to download this book. **It has helped me tons** and I recommend it for anyone [who] suffers from procrastination."
~ Steven Dana Scobey

"**This is a great manual on how to improve your every day productivity**...The book gives very useful tips [that are] easy-to-follow and effective in their application."

~ Rosalinda Scalia

CONTENTS

YOUR FREE GIFT

As a way of saying thank you for your purchase, I'd like to offer you a free bonus package worth $297. This bonus package contains eBooks, videos and audiotapes on how to overcome procrastination and triple your productivity. You can download the free bonus here:
www.AkashKaria.com/FREE

For Chloe Sha,
Because you inspire me to be the best that I can be.

INTRODUCTION

STOP PROCRASTINATING AND START GETTING THINGS DONE

Do you find yourself often putting things off till "tomorrow"?

That book you wanted to write? "Tomorrow".

That email you're supposed to send? "Tomorrow".

That project you said you'd start yesterday? "Tomorrow".

Packed with twenty-three tools on how to stop procrastinating, get motivated and start getting things done, *"Ready, Set, Procrastinate!"* will prove to be an indispensible resource for those who want to get the most out life.

DEVELOP THE "NOW" HABIT

If you want to stop dreaming and start doing, you must develop the "now" habit. This book will show you how to do just that. In it, you will learn how to:

- **Tackle any task using the solar-flaring technique.**

- Complete large, complex tasks using the Lego block technique.

- **Trick yourself into working on any project using the five-minute technique.**

- Eliminate procrastinator-talk using a simple eight-step method.

- **Instantly increase your motivation using two simple words.**

- Tackle perfectionist thoughts that cause you to procrastinate.

- **Beat procrastination using Dan Ariely's simple trick.**

- Make inherently boring tasks more interesting.

- **Create positive new habits using the Seinfeld calendar.**
- Stop conveniently "forgetting" painful tasks.

- **Instantly eliminate disguised procrastination using the Pareto principle.**

- Dramatically cut how much time you waste online.

- **Use the 'if-then' technique to triple your chances of success.**

- Use pre-commitment devices to lock your future self into your desired course of action.

- **Triple your productivity using a simple time-management technique and a kitchen timer.**

Ready? Set? GO!

CHAPTER ONE

THE PROCRASTINATOR'S GUIDE TO GETTING THINGS DONE

Have you ever fallen into the trap of putting things off till tomorrow? Telling yourself that you'll start on that project "tomorrow"? That you'll write that book "tomorrow"? That you'll send out that email "tomorrow"?

The words "tomorrow" and "later" are the enemies of successful people. Over the past five years that I've spent researching the science of success, I've discovered that **successful people have an ability to "get things done" – even when they don't feel like doing them.**

HOW PROCRASTINATION GOT ME DEPORTED OUT OF A COUNTRY

For a long period of my life, I struggled with procrastination. I procrastinated so much in college that I ended up with rock-bottom grades. I procrastinated for two years before I finally wrote my first book. And I even procrastinated so long on renewing my tourist visa that I was deported out of

Malaysia (seriously, if you're traveling in Malaysia – or traveling anywhere, for that matter – make sure you extend your tourist visa if you plan on staying longer than the allowed entry period!). To put it in simple terms, I'm an expert at procrastinating!

What's interesting about procrastinating is that **you *always* find ways of justifying why things should be put off till "tomorrow."** When I procrastinated on my college assignments, I always justified doing so by telling myself things such as "I'll be better prepared tomorrow" or "I'm not feeling motivated, so it's better to wait till I'm feeling energized tomorrow."

Can you think of a time when you procrastinated on something important? Perhaps you put off paying your insurance premium? Or perhaps you put off a work-related project till the last minute? What excuses did you use to justify your actions (or failure to act lack, rather)?

WHAT PROCRASTINATION IS COSTING YOU

In an article in the *New Yorker,* James Surowiecki writes about the cost of procrastination:

> "Each year, Americans waste hundreds of millions of dollars because they don't file their taxes on time. **The Harvard economist David Laibson has shown that American workers have forgone huge amounts of money in matching 401(k)**

contributions because they never got around to signing up for a retirement plan. Seventy per cent of patients suffering from glaucoma risk blindness because they don't use their eyedrops regularly. Procrastination also inflicts major costs on businesses and governments. The recent crisis of the euro was exacerbated by the German government's dithering, and the decline of the American auto industry, exemplified by the bankruptcy of G.M., was due in part to executives' penchant for delaying tough decisions." – via New Yorker (*www.bit.ly/ny-procrastination*)

Given that procrastinating carries such high costs, why do so many of us do it anyway? Are *you* procrastinating on something that you *know* you should be doing? How is procrastination impacting your life (socially, financially, spiritually, emotionally)? How much better would your life be if you were able to beat procrastination and get things done?

In this short guide, I will walk you through the root causes of procrastination and equip you with **simple yet practical tools that will help you avoid procrastination.**

Of course, you never really "win" the war against procrastination. Overcoming procrastination is not a one-time fight. Procrastination is a tough enemy – you're always fighting it, every single day. You never ever really "conquer" it. However, with the tools covered in this little guide, you will be able to give yourself a fighting chance.

STOP DREAMING AND START DOING

Whether you've been putting off paying your bills or writing the book that you've always talked about, you can increase your odds of getting things done by using the tools you'll discover in this book.

How can I be so confident? Because these are the same tools that I've used to write 11 books while maintaining a full-time job as the chief commercial officer for a multimillion-dollar company. I've managed to overcome my laziness and make going to the gym a daily activity. And yes, whenever I travel, I now renew my tourist visa at least a week in advance!

The tools you will read about in this book are based **on my experiences as an expert procrastinator as well as the hundreds of hours of research** I have spent studying anti-procrastination techniques.

If you want to learn how to stop dreaming and start doing – if you want to stop putting things off and start getting things done – then this little book is your roadmap to success.

Let's get started...

CHAPTER TWO

THE SOLAR FLARING TECHNIQUE FOR AVOIDING PROCRASTINATION

Think of a large project that you recently procrastinated on – perhaps it was preparing your company's annual report; or perhaps it was filling out your tax forms; or perhaps it was writing your book. Write it down below:

Work out   get passport
_____
_____
_____
_____

Whatever large project or task you've procrastinated on, it's likely that one of the reasons you procrastinated (consciously or unconsciously) was because you **dreaded getting started**.

Why? Because the task was too big and intimidating. Or because it was just boring and you couldn't imagine putting yourself through the several hours of boredom it would take to complete it. You looked at how long it would take you to complete it, and as a result you dreaded even getting started.

HOW NEWTON'S FIRST LAW OF MOTION ALSO APPLIES TO PROCRASTINATION

If you've studied high school physics, you've most likely heard of Newton's first law of motion. I'm not going to challenge your memory by asking you to recall it, but here's what it says: "An object at rest stays at rest unless acted upon by an external force. Similarly, an object in motion stays in motion unless acted upon by an external force." (My high school physics did come in useful after all. My teacher would be so proud!)

So, what has Newton's law got to do with procrastination? Great question. You see, Newton's law can also be applied to procrastination. If you're procrastinating on a project, you're like an object at rest – not making any progress and very unlikely to do so in the future.

From my vast experience in procrastination, I've found that **when you say you'll work on a project "tomorrow," you're also likely to put it off tomorrow.**

However, if you *get started* on your project (even if it's a small start), you become an object in motion, and you will continue being in motion and making progress on your project. **People who *start* on a task or project are more likely to continue working on it – and will often work** on it for a longer period of time than they planned to do.

THE PUZZLE STUDY (& PROOF RESEARCHERS ARE EVIL)

In one research study conducted by Greist-Bousquet and Schiffman (*www.bit.ly/schiffman-study*), the researchers gave the participants some puzzles to complete. Imagine that you're one of the participants in this study. You've been given some "brain-buster" puzzles to complete, but here's the catch: You haven't been given enough time to complete them (researchers are evil!).

So, what happens when the researcher says that time's up? Do you stop working on your puzzle and simply get up and leave? Or do you stay behind to finish off the puzzles even though you don't have to?

It turns out that **over 90% of the participants in the study went on to complete the puzzle anyway!** What this shows is that people have a tendency to complete what they start. As Newton's first law states, "An object in motion will continue staying in motion (unless acted upon by an external force)."

OK, now that you know *getting started* is the key to beating procrastination, how do you go about motivating yourself to get started?

After all, procrastination means that you *don't want to get started*, so how do you go from being "at rest" to being "in motion"?

Here's where the solar flaring technique comes in...

THE SOLAR FLARING TECHNIQUE

"What's the solar flaring technique?" you ask. First of all, isn't that such a cool name for an anti-procrastination technique? I'm a sucker for great concepts with cool names!

Unfortunately I wasn't the one who coined the term. I came across the concept on a site called "Asian Efficiency" (*www.AsianEfficiency.com*) and it's a very simple but effective concept that can help you overcome procrastination.

In order to understand what the solar flaring technique is, you first need to understand what a solar flare is. A solar flare is a star explosion that starts off very small but then grows MASSIVE.

The solar flaring method (when applied to procrastination) is similar: It refers to **starting off by working on a very small piece of the task** you've been dreading (for example, writing only the first sentence of your book). However, the momentum you gain from starting your task gives you a new burst of energy and allows you to go on to tackle more and more of the project.

Here's an example: Let's say that your goal is to go jogging every morning. However, when the alarm rings at 6 a.m., the thought of running around the block in your sleep-deprived state is too dreadful, so you hit the snooze button and head back to bed. A couple of hours later, when you're awake, you're filled with guilt and tell yourself that "tomorrow" you'll wake up and go for a jog.

Unfortunately, I've experienced this particular scenario hundreds of times. However, once I used the solar flaring technique, things changed. Here's what I did: Because the thought of exercising early in the morning was too dreadful, I told myself that I would wake up at 6 a.m. and put on my tracksuit and sneakers. **My goal was no longer to go for a jog around the block – it was to tackle a small part of the task, which was simply to put on my running gear.**

After that, I gave myself permission to go back to bed if I wanted to – and on some days, I did! However, on most days, I ended up not only putting on my running gear, but also going for a jog because I'd already put on my tracksuit and sneakers.

I've applied the solar flaring technique to virtually every area of my life – whenever I experience some kind of dread at getting started, I look for a **ridiculously small first step** that I *know* I can summon enough willpower to take.

Writing my book becomes "write one sentence." Going to the gym becomes "put on my gym gear."

Going to sleep early becomes "turn off the lights."

Once I take the ridiculously small first step, I find that it becomes much easier to put one foot in front of another, and pretty soon I end up making more progress on the task than I'd imagined.

THE FIVE-MINUTE TECHNIQUE

Another great technique to help you get started on your task is called the "five-minute technique." As the name of the technique implies, all you do here is **commit yourself to working on your chosen task for just five minutes.**

One of the reasons we procrastinate is because we dread spending *hours* working on a task we don't like. The very thought of working on the task for a long period of time (e.g., doing the taxes, cleaning out the garage, preparing the annual company report) tires us out. It saps away our mental energy. Thus, we make excuses such as "I'll do it tomorrow when I have more time" or "I'm too tired right now, so I'll save it for tomorrow." I'm ashamed to admit that these are both excuses I have made far too often.

Fortunately, there's a solution. **The five-minute technique helps decrease the perceived pain of working on the task.** It's painful to think about working on an unpleasant task for two hours, but it's much easier to think about doing it for only five minutes.

Therefore, here's what I want you to do: *I want you to commit yourself to working on your chosen task for just five minutes.* This eliminates all excuses such as not having enough time or not having enough energy – after all, it's only five minutes!

Next, get a countdown timer and set it to five minutes. Once the timer starts ticking, work on your chosen task until your five minutes are up. At the end of the five minutes, you're free to let yourself off the hook and go do something more pleasant.

Come back the next day and use the five-minute technique again. This builds the foundation for a habit where you stop putting things off and start getting things done (even if it's only for five minutes). This habit will serve you very well in the long term.

However, what's most likely to happen at the end of your five minutes is that you'll continue working on the task for longer than you expected.

Why?

Because even though the task may have seemed intimidating and dreadful, once we get started on the task we realize that it's not as bad as it seemed. That was the conclusion Timothy A. Pychyl, from Carleton University in Canada, came to after conducting a series of tests. In the test, the participants received random messages during the day over a period of two weeks. These messages asked the participants to report how they were feeling and whether or not they should have been working on anything else at that moment.

"I WISH I'D STARTED EARLIER..."

Pychyl's research revealed that before the participants engaged in the tasks they should have been doing, they saw these tasks as problematic and unpleasant. As a result, the participants put off doing the tasks for as long as they could.

However, **once the participants started working on the tasks, they reported that they found the tasks interesting or engaging and wished they had begun earlier.** In other words, the tasks weren't as bad as they had seemed.

Have you ever had the same experience – the experience that once you started working on your task, you realized that it was actually OK (or goodness, even interesting!) and you wished you'd started on it earlier?

THE KEY TO AVOIDING PROCRASTINATION...

The key to beating procrastination and getting things done is to reduce the pain associated with the task. One way to do this is by using the solar flaring method, where you break the task down into the most ridiculously simple first step you can take, and then take that first step.

Alternatively, you can use the five-minute method to get started. Once you begin making progress on your task, you'll find that the task isn't as bad as it seemed and you'll most likely make more progress on it than you'd initially expected.

IN A NUTSHELL

- The key to avoiding procrastination is reducing the dread and pain associated with the task.

- Research reveals that once people get started working on a task, they have a tendency to want to complete it.

- Tasks that seem boring and intimidating before people start working on them are seen as engaging and interesting once people start doing them.

- The solar flaring technique involves breaking a task into a ridiculously small first step and then focusing on working on only that first step.

- The five-minute technique eliminates the dread associated with a task as well as the excuse that you don't have any time.

- Use the solar flaring and/or the five-minute technique every day to make small amounts of progress on your chosen tasks. This will help set the foundation for a positive habit.

ACTIONABLE KNOWLEDGE

APPLICATION EXERCISE #1

1 – Choose one important task that you *know* you should get done but have been putting off for a long time. Write it down below:

Working out

2 – **Solar Flaring Technique:** Break the above task into the ridiculously smallest first step you can take (e.g., if your task is "clean up the garage," the ridiculously simple first step would be "Go to the garage and throw away two pieces of junk"). Write that step down below:

wear sneakers tie hair
up gym shorts

3 – **Five-Minute Technique:** Commit yourself to working on your task for just five minutes. Grab a countdown timer and set it to five minutes. Once the timer starts counting down, work on the task you've been putting off until the five minutes are up.

If, after the five minutes are up, you'd like to continue working longer, go ahead. If not, come back the next day and use the solar flaring technique or the five-minute technique (or a combination of both) to continue working on the task. This will help you build the foundation for a positive habit.

CHAPTER THREE

THE LEGO BLOCK TECHNIQUE

Have you ever looked at a large task looming ahead of you and been intimidated by the sheer size of it? Or has the complexity of a task ever confused you?

While the solar-flaring technique helps you *get started* on simple, straightforward tasks (but admittedly ones that you don't want to do), sometimes getting started may not be enough – especially when the **root cause of your procrastination lies in the fact that you're intimidated by the complexity of the task ahead.**

SIMPLE VS. COMPLEX TASKS

Let me give you an example: Writing a book is a fairly straightforward task. Using the solar-flaring technique, I'm able to overcome my laziness and "get into the groove" and write a substantial amount.

However, when it comes to creating the annual report for my company, the root cause of the problem is not that I'm lazy (as I am when it comes to writing), but that the task is immensely complex. I have to analyze sales figures, salary expenses, administrative expenses, asset acquisition data, cash flow figures, forecasted sales and expense data as well as hundreds of other numbers (all the while making sure that self-reported figures from department heads match up with those from the accounting department).

Given that I work in a multimillion-dollar company with several products and huge investments in various sectors, you can see why this can be such a challenging task – and why I'd want to put it off. While the solar flaring technique helps me get started, **I soon become frustrated because the project is too complex – and I end up putting if off for another day.**

So, what's the solution?

HOW TO STOP PROCRASTINATING ON LARGE, COMPLEX TASKS

I call the solution the "Lego block" technique. Why? Because it's similar to building a Lego blockhouse.

As a child, how did you build a Lego blockhouse? You did it one block at a time. And while that sounds corny (and it is), it's also true. The same principle applies to getting things done. You should not attempt to tackle a large, complicated task all at once. **Tackle it one block at a time.** Trying to do otherwise will result in your brain serving you a host of legitimate excuses such as "I don't have enough time" or "I'll have more energy to do this tomorrow."

To apply the Lego block technique, here's what you need to do:

1 – Write down the task you need to complete (e.g., "create annual company report").

2 – Break the task down into a step-by-step list of its smallest subcomponents (e.g., "get sales data from the head of sales," "create line chart showing sales trends," "ask the accounts department for data on company expenses").

3 – Schedule time to work on each block separately.

By focusing on each block individually, you avoid the dread and intimidation that come with tackling a large project. Furthermore, **by breaking a complex task into its smaller components, you're able to avoid the confusion and complexity that come with handling a large task.** Finally, the very act of breaking a large project down into its smallest parts clarifies the scope of what you need to do and how you need to do it.

If you ever find yourself procrastinating because you are intimidated by the size of a task or confused by its complexity, use the Lego block technique (along with the solar flaring method and the five-minute technique) to help you get started.

IN A NUTSHELL

- Sometimes the root cause of procrastination is not that we are lazy, but that the task is too complex or large for us to handle all at once.

- Use the Lego block technique to break large, complex tasks into their smallest subcomponents ("blocks") and work on one block at a time.

ACTIONABLE KNOWLEDGE

APPLICATION EXERCISE #2

1 – Think of a task or a project that you're putting off because you're intimidated by its sheer size or complexity. Write it down below:

_____

_____

_____

_____

_____

_____

_____

2 – Break the task into the smallest possible subcomponents that you can. Completing a large task is the result of a lot of smaller actions. Write all those tasks/action steps below.

_____

_____

_____

_____

_____

_____

_____

3 – Organize those action steps ("blocks") into a logical, step-by-step, numbered to-do list.

_____

_____

_____

_____

_____

_____

_____

4 – Next to each task ("block") on your to-do list, schedule a specific time that you will work on that task (e.g., "Saturday, 7:30–7:45 p.m.). This makes it more likely that you'll complete that task on the given day instead of putting it off till some imaginary "tomorrow."

CHAPTER FOUR

HOW TO AVOID PROCRASTINATOR TALK

Never doubt the importance of language when it comes to procrastination. In fact, unless you take control of your inner dialogue, it's unlikely that you'll ever be able to make the commitment to stop procrastinating or use any of the tools covered in this book!

WHAT PROCRASTINATORS SAY WHEN THEY TALK TO THEMSELVES

Think of a time that you were procrastinating on something important. Now, try to remember what you said to yourself before you decided to put the task off till later. Most likely you were talking like a procrastinator, making excuses such as:

- "I don't have enough time today, so I might as well do this tomorrow."

- "Because I'm feeling tired today, it's best if I save this till later."

- "I work better under tight deadlines, so I'll wait until the day before the deadline to get started."

- "It's already too late, so I'd rather wait till tomorrow."

All of these are excuses are what I call "procrastinator talk." On the surface, these excuses seem perfectly logical. They make sense! But that's the scary thing about procrastination – **it's very easy to justify it**, and unless we take control of it, we'll always find ourselves completing tasks close to the deadline and experiencing the high stress associated with doing so.

From my study of successful people, I've found that **successful people have a habit of getting things done NOW!** They take action, even when they're feeling tired or don't have enough time or enough energy (after all, who has enough time or enough energy?). Why wait till tomorrow when you can do it today?

WHAT PRODUCTIVE, SUCCESSFUL PEOPLE SAY WHEN THEY TALK TO THEMSELVES

Instead of using procrastinator talk, successful people use "productivity talk." They say to themselves things such as:

- "Why put it off till tomorrow when it can be done today?"

- "Even though I'm feeling tired, I'll make a little progress on this today so that I have less to do tomorrow."

- "It's better to do make some progress today rather than wait till tomorrow to get started."

- "I'll never have enough time or energy, so the best time to get started is now."

- "Tomorrow I'll wish I'd started today."

HOW TO CHANGE PROCRASTINATOR TALK TO PRODUCTIVITY TALK

To change procrastinator talk to productivity talk, here's a simple step-by-step system you can use (I've used this successfully to stop negative thinking as well as overcome procrastinator talk):

1 – Look at how much your procrastinator talk is costing you. How much stress are you experiencing as a result of procrastinating? How is leaving things till the last minute impacting the quality of your work?

2 – Imagine how your life would be if you stopped procrastinating. How would it benefit your career? Your finances? Your personal life? How much better would your life be if you built a habit of getting things done instead of putting them off till "later"?

Note: The previous two steps will cause you to become uncomfortable, which is exactly what is required if you want to make a change in your life. **Comfort is the enemy of change. Being uncomfortable is what leads to action and to positive change.**

3 – When you find yourself procrastinating, monitor your inner dialogue. What excuses (and yes, no matter how logical they seem, they are EXCUSES) are you giving yourself?

4 – Question your procrastinator talk. If you find yourself saying, "I don't have enough time," ask yourself, "Is this really true? Don't I even have five minutes to work on this task?"

5 – Accept that you are using excuses to procrastinate. Realize that, no matter how logical the excuses seem to you, they are just excuses that are preventing you from completing your task.

6 – Replace procrastinator talk with productivity talk. When you find yourself saying things such as "It's better to do this tomorrow when I have a bit more energy," replace that with productivity talk (e.g., "It's better to make a small amount of progress now than to make no progress at all"). Remember, **tomorrow you'll wish you'd started today!**

7 – Take **immediate action** to justify your productivity talk. Once you make use of one of the productivity-talk statements, immediately take some form of action to justify

it. Work on your task at least five minutes. **Doing this will begin to change your self-image**. You will go from seeing yourself as someone who procrastinates to someone who gets things done!

8 – Keep repeating the above steps. Over time, your procrastinator talk will be replaced by productivity talk and you'll find you have become a doer instead of just a dreamer.

IN A NUTSHELL

- What you say to yourself affects how you see yourself as well as the decisions that you make.

- When you find yourself procrastinating, monitor your inner dialogue.

- Reject procrastinator talk by rejecting excuses for procrastination.

- Replace procrastinator talk with productivity talk.

- Take immediate action to justify your productivity talk.

ACTIONABLE KNOWLEDGE

APPLICATION EXERCISE #3

1 – What are some of the common excuses you use to justify procrastination? Write down your top three excuses below:

I dont have time

Im tired

Tomorrow I'll be prepared

2 – Create some responses you can use to fight back against these procrastination statements (e.g., "Telling myself I don't have enough time means I'll never get it done because I won't ever have enough time!"). Write at least one response below:

I have 5 minutes

Im always tired mine as well be productive

Theres no day like today

3 – Create some productivity dialogues you can use to replace your procrastinator talk with productivity talk (e.g., "It's better to make even five minutes of progress now than to wait till tomorrow to get started."). Write at least one dialogue below:

Its better to get started now then to not do any cut all

4 – When you catch yourself procrastinating, fight back against your excuses and replace the procrastination talk with the productivity dialogues you have prepared

CHAPTER FIVE

THE "WILL I?" TECHNIQUE

Have you ever told yourself that you were going to do something, but then failed to do it?

For example, you told yourself, "I'm going to go to the gym tomorrow," but when tomorrow rolled around, you didn't go?

Or perhaps you told yourself, "I'm going to call my in-laws tonight," and then didn't call? (Of course, who can blame you?)

WHY YOU SHOULDN'T TELL YOURSELF YOU'RE GOING TO DO SOMETHING

If you're anything like me, you break promises to yourself a bit too often. But don't feel too bad. It turns out that telling yourself you're going to do something isn't the best strategy for getting yourself to do it. Here's an interesting piece of research that proves this (conducted by Dolores Albarracín at the University of Illinois):

"Albarracin's team tested this kind of motivation in 50 study participants, encouraging them explicitly to either spend a minute wondering whether they would complete a task or telling themselves they would. **The participants showed more success on an anagram task, rearranging set words to create different words, when they asked themselves whether they would complete it than when they told themselves they would.**

Further experimentation had students in a seemingly unrelated task simply write two ostensibly unrelated sentences, either "I Will" or "Will I," and then work on the same task. **Participants did better when they wrote, "Will" followed by "I"** even though they had no idea that the word writing related to the anagram task." – via Eurekalert (*www.bit.ly/eureka-study*)

Wow, isn't that interesting? If you want to increase your odds of doing something, ask yourself whether you will do it instead of telling yourself that you will.

For example, if I want to work on my book, I ask myself, "Will I work on my book tonight?" (as opposed to telling myself, "I will work on my book tonight," which is what I previously used to do).

Sure, asking yourself whether you are going to do something feels strange at first, but it does build your intrinsic motivation to do it.

When I ask myself whether I'm going to work on my book, I follow up with "Yes, I'll go ahead and work on the book after I finish eating dinner." Asking myself the question of whether I will do something forces me to work through the scenario and mentally plan ahead for how I will do it (which then increases my chances of doing so). Telling yourself you are going to do something doesn't allow room for this kind of introspection.

Next time you want to get something done, use the words "Will I" instead of "I will." Of course, this simple technique will not transform you from chronic procrastinator to productivity master overnight, but it is a cool little tip that will (as indicated by the research) increase your chances of getting things done.

For a tip that takes virtually no effort and relies on changing the order of two words, I think that's a good deal!

IN A NUTSHELL

- Telling yourself you will do something is not as powerful as asking yourself whether you will.

- To increase intrinsic motivation, use the words "Will I" instead of "I will."

ACTIONABLE KNOWLEDGE

APPLICATION EXERCISE #4

1 – What task would you like to get accomplished tonight? Instead of telling yourself you will get it accomplished, write it down as a question using the words "Will I?"

Will i work out?

2 – If your answer to the above question is a "Yes," notice how your mind goes through an examination process of *how* you will do it. Go ahead and write down the plan your brain comes up with (e.g., "Will I go to the gym today?" Answer: "Yes, I will at 6 p.m. after I get out of work.").

Yes, tonight in the livingroom

CHAPTER SIX

HOW TO USE THE SEINFELD CALENDAR

The Seinfeld calendar is a super-cool technique that will help you overcome your procrastination habit. It'll also help you make daily progress towards your goals and dreams.

Once you learn it, you'll beat yourself over the head for not having used it sooner (plus, it's so simple that you'll wonder why you didn't think of it!).

NO TOOL TO HOLD YOU ACCOUNTABLE

One of the reasons we procrastinate is because we don't have any self-monitoring tool. We tell ourselves we'll work on that project tomorrow, and three days go by and we've done nothing. A couple more days go by and the project moves to the back of our mind (it's still there, but we don't really pay any attention to it).

HOW A CALENDAR CAN MOTIVATE YOU TO START GETTING THINGS DONE

Let's say that you have a big project that you're working on – something that will take you at least a week or more to complete. The best way to tackle this project would be to make some daily progress towards completing small blocks of it instead of leaving it all to the last day.

However, it's **easy to procrastinate frequently when you don't have a tool to monitor how frequently you've been procrastinating**. What if you had a tool that would allow you to monitor how often you've been procrastinating? Would that increase your motivation to stop procrastinating and get things done? I'm betting it would!

This is where the Seinfeld calendar comes into play. The technique is named after Jerry Seinfeld, who is one of the most successful comedians of all time. Here's my adapted version of how it works:

1 – Split your large tasks into smaller blocks (the Lego block technique).

2 – Calculate how many days you have to complete the entire task and assign the blocks to each day.

3 – Grab a calendar and purchase a marker.

4 – Hang the calendar in a prominent place where you have no choice but to see it everyday (your bathroom and your bedroom are two great options).

5 – When you make progress and complete the tasks assigned on the scheduled days, cross off each day on the calendar with a big fat X. Soon, you will begin to create a chain of X's. Your job is to ensure that you do not break that chain.

As Jerry Seinfeld says, "You'll like seeing that chain, especially when you get a few weeks under your belt. Your only job now is to not break the chain."

While this technique is very simple, it has proven very useful for me. As a writer, it's easy for me to procrastinate because I don't have anyone watching over me. However, with the Seinfeld calendar, I have been able to track how many days I put off writing till "tomorrow." Having this data in a place where I cannot miss it **makes me uncomfortable with procrastinating** and is usually enough to give me the burst of motivation I need to get off my butt and get started.

If you want to kick the procrastination habit and become a doer, then the Seinfeld calendar is a great tool to implement! Try it out and you'll find that it will motivate you to stop putting things off and get things done!

IN A NUTSHELL

- It's easy to procrastinate when you don't monitor how frequently you've been procrastinating.

- The Seinfeld calendar is a great way to keep yourself accountable for those days when you do procrastinate.

- Not only will the Seinfeld calendar make procrastinating uncomfortable, it will also motivate you as you begin to build up a chain of X's on it.

ACTIONABLE KNOWLEDGE

APPLICATION EXERCISE #5

1 – Buy a calendar and hang it in a prominent place in your home.

2 – Choose a task that will take you at least several days to complete (and one that you've been procrastinating on for some time). Write the task below:

Clean the house I nanny for

3 – Whenever you work that task, even if it is just for five minutes ("five-minute technique"), mark the day with a big X. Your job is to create an unbroken chain of X's.

CHAPTER SEVEN

HOW TO CHANGE TASK ASSOCIATIONS

According to motivational guru Anthony Robbins, people are motivated by two things: pain and pleasure. They will do anything they can to avoid pain and they will work hard to receive pleasure. When you think about this pain-pleasure principle in terms of procrastination, you can see that it makes sense:

Why do you put off doing your taxes? Because you associate it with pain.

Why do you put off cleaning up your attic? Because you associate it with pain.

Why do you watch TV when you know you should be working? Because watching TV gives you pleasure whereas working causes you pain.

If you're putting something off, it's probably because you associate some kind of pain with it. **You view it as being unpleasant, and therefore to avoid that pain, you avoid that task!**

DAN ARIELY'S SIMPLE TRICK FOR BEATING PROCRASTINATION

The trick to beating procrastination is to stop associating the task with pain and associate it instead with some kind of reward. This reward will motivate you to complete the task. By changing the association you have with the task, you'll become much more likely to engage in it.

As an example, consider how Dan Ariely (a psychology professor at Duke University) used this principle (he recounts this particular story in his best-selling book, *Predictably Irrational*). When Ariely was infected with hepatitis C, he was told that in order to cure the infection he would have to inject himself with interferon.

Injecting yourself with interferon is no walk in the park – the side effects involve fever, vomiting and dizziness. Ariely's medication scheduled involved him injecting himself with interferon three days a week for a period of eighteen months. Most patients given this treatment are unable to stick to their medication regimen, and you can see why!

So, how did Ariely fare? At the end of the eighteen months, his doctors said he was the only one of their patients who'd managed to take the medication regularly.

How did Ariely manage, when it would have been so easy to skip a couple of days? He did this by changing his associations with the medication. **Because he loved movies, he rewarded himself with watching his favorite**

movies on the days that he injected himself with interferon. This reward was a strong enough motivator to keep him on track with his medication schedule.

HOW TO CHANGE YOUR ASSOCIATIONS TO A TASK

So, how do you apply this principle to your own life? By finding ways to reward yourself for doing things that you don't like. Change the association to a task. Instead of associating the task with pain, associate it with some kind of pleasure. Here's how you can do that:

1 – Choose a reward that you love. It should be something that you value so much that the pleasure of the reward outweighs the pain of the task you have to complete.

2 – Think about how great it will be to enjoy the reward. Imagine how much pleasure you will experience when you are enjoying the reward. Get yourself into a state where you are *excited* about the reward.

3 – Tie the reward to the completion of the task. Tell yourself that you can enjoy the reward only if you complete the task that you've been procrastinating on.

4 – When you complete the said task, enjoy your reward! You deserve it.

5 – If you fail to work on the task, punish yourself by withholding the reward. It's essential that you don't allow yourself to enjoy the reward until you complete the task. Also, examine why you failed to complete the task. Perhaps you need to change the reward so that the pull of the reward is stronger. **If the reward is irresistible enough, you'll push yourself through any pain to achieve it.**

IN A NUTSHELL

- People procrastinate on tasks that they view as being painful.

- To stop procrastinating on a task, attach its completion to a reward you value highly.

- When you complete the task, reward yourself to build positive associations to the task.

- If you fail to complete the task, withhold the reward to punish yourself for procrastinating.

ACTIONABLE KNOWLEDGE

APPLICATION EXERCISE #6

1 – Choose an unpleasant task you need to complete and set a clear, measurable goal that you would like to achieve (e.g., "work for one hour on my presentation" or "write the first chapter of my book" or "exercise for 30 minutes"). Write the task below:

Exercise

2 – Work on changing your association with the task. To do this, find a reward that is pleasurable enough to motivate you to complete the task. Tell yourself that you can enjoy the reward only if you complete (or make a measurable amount of progress) on the task. Write your desired reward below:

Phone time

3 – If you do achieve your set goal, allow yourself to enjoy the reward. If not, withhold the reward to associate pain with procrastination.

4 – Repeat this process often for ongoing tasks (e.g., writing, going to the gym, studying) to change your perceived association with the task.

CHAPTER EIGHT

HOW TO MAKE INHERENTLY BORING TASKS MORE INTERESTING

As we saw in the last chapter, you're going to find it difficult to engage in any activity if you associate it with pain. If you view the task as boring, dull and uninteresting, it's no wonder that you're procrastinating!

Tying the task to a reward is a great technique for motivating yourself to get started on the task, but there's an even more powerful technique. Here's the technique: **Make the task fun!** This may sound very simple and trite, but it works!

So, how do you make an inherently boring task fun?

There are several ways I make the task I am working on more interesting. Now, before you read further, I realize that not all of these techniques will be relevant to you. Take what you find useful, apply it to your life and discard the rest. With that being said, here's how I make boring work more interesting:

1 – CHANGE ENVIRONMENTS

If possible, change the environment to one that is fun and interesting. For example, when I find myself procrastinating on my writing or doing financial analysis for my company, I get out of my house and head over to my favorite café.

Being in a café automatically makes whatever task I am working on more enjoyable. I love the smell of coffee and the quiet chatter of people.

By the way, speaking of cafés, research has revealed that the sounds at a coffee shop boost creativity. Here's the research:

> "In a series of experiments that looked at the effects of noise on creative thinking, researchers at the University of Illinois at Urbana-Champaign had participants brainstorm ideas for new products while they were exposed to varying levels of background noise. Their results, published in The Journal of Consumer Research, found that **a level of ambient noise typical of a bustling coffee shop or a television playing in a living room, about 70 decibels, enhanced performance compared with the relative quiet of 50 decibels.**

> A higher level of noise, however, about 85 decibels, roughly the noise level generated by a blender or a garbage disposal, was too distracting, the researchers found." – via New York Times

What environments do you enjoy being in?

Here's another example: For a long time, I had wanted to make swimming a regular part of my day. However, I'm not a fan of swimming! I hate being in cold water. I had been telling myself I would start swimming but putting it off day after day. I had even signed up for a gym with an indoor swimming pool but never actually went there.

So, to make swimming more fun, I chose a gym with an outdoor swimming pool that had an AMAZING view of the ocean.

The view was so gorgeous that I found myself wanting to go the gym just so that I could enjoy the beautiful sunset after work. Once there, I would get into the pool and swim, allowing myself to admire the view between laps. After my swimming session, I would reward myself with a delicious but healthy dinner.

Of course, changing environments might not be possible for you if your goal is to clean up your garage. However, if possible, try changing your environment. Sometimes that can be all it takes to get started on a task that you've been putting off.

2 – ADD SOME MUSIC

When I'm forced to do some really boring work (such as cleaning up my home), I make the task more interesting by playing some music. Because I enjoy music, the chore of cleaning up my home goes from being deadly dull to being a more pleasurable experience where I get to listen to my favorite songs. Some of my friends also use this technique when they go to the gym or go jogging: By listening to good music on their iPods, they make the experience of working out more pleasurable.

Similarly, I write with some light, instrumental music in the background. According to the website *Ooomf*:

> "When you listen to music, a part of your brain called the nucleus accumbens activates. This triggers the release of the 'pleasure chemical' dopamine, that lives in a group of neurons in your brain called the Ventral Tegmental Area (VTA): This pathway in the brain is called the Reward System and Dopamine is strongly associated with it." – via Ooomf

Published studies also note the effect of music on task improvement:

> "In a study published in the journal of Neuroscience of Behavior and Physiology, it was found that a person's ability to recognize images, letters, and numbers was faster when rock or classical music was playing in the background compared to when there was no music.

> A similar effect was noted when workers on an assembly line listened to music. The workers who

listened to music were more happy and efficient and made fewer errors.

So whatever type of music you like, as long as you're listening to something, you'll enjoy repetitive or boring tasks more and get them done faster." – via Ooomf

The important thing when choosing music to listen to is to ensure that it's music that you're familiar with so that it doesn't distract you. Also, instrumental music is best because songs with lyrics can distract you from thinking (you might suddenly find yourself signing the lyrics instead).

The next time you get stuck writing, try adding some familiar instrumental music into the mix to help get your creative juices flowing.

3 – TURN THE TASK INTO A SOCIAL ACTIVITY

When my girlfriend was studying for her CFA examinations, we made the experience enjoyable by working together. By chatting and joking around during our scheduled breaks, we were able to turn a dull study session into something more fun.

I've also used this technique to improve my fitness levels. When I was in boarding school, I knew that I needed to improve my fitness levels but found it difficult to wake up at 6 a.m. and go for a run.

However, when I bounced the idea off my roommate, he was very enthusiastic about it and proposed we start running together, which we did. We would wake up every morning at 6 a.m. and go for a run together. The social aspect of running made exercising more enjoyable than running alone.

Not only are tasks more enjoyable when you turn them into a social activity, you also get accountability partners who will encourage you when you feel like quitting.

How can you add a social element to your activity?

4 – GET CREATIVE

The previous tips might or might not work for you, but the point is that you should try different methods to make your task more interesting. For example, a friend of mine has found a creative way to stop procrastinating and start cleaning up her house. She makes the task of cleaning up her house more enjoyable by turning it into a game. She keeps a record of how long it takes her to clean her house and uses a stopwatch to beat her previous time.

It sounds strange, but it's a creative way that works for her!

When you are looking at a task that you've been putting off for some time, **ask yourself, "How can I make this more interesting or enjoyable?"** Don't be afraid to experiment with wild and creative strategies – in fact, the wilder and more creative your idea, the more likely it is that you will be excited to get started.

IN A NUTSHELL

- If you want to stop procrastinating, then try making the task more fun.

- Changing environments can sometimes be all it takes to stop procrastinating.

- If you enjoy music, try adding music to the task to make it more pleasurable.

- Turning the task into a social activity is another great option for making a task more interesting.

- Keep experimenting with new and creative ways to make boring tasks more exciting.

ACTIONABLE KNOWLEDGE

APPLICATION EXERCISE #7

Write down some creative ideas you can use to make your task more fun and interesting. The more fun your task is, the less likely you are to procrastinate.

work out w/ the kids
play music

CHAPTER NINE

THE PERFECTIONIST'S CURSE

One of the reasons it took me two years to write my first book was because I had extremely high expectations of it. I wanted it to be PERFECT (yep, PERFECT in capitals). I didn't just want it to be a *good* book; I wanted it to be the best book on public speaking. I wanted it to be the ultimate in public speaking resources.

I had dreams making it a New York Times bestseller and receiving rave reviews from the likes of Seth Godin, Robert Kiyosaki and Anthony Robbins.

HOW MY PURSUIT FOR PERFECTION LED TO PROCRASTINATION

However, after almost one and a half years of no progress, I was getting frustrated. I had such high expectations of my writing that I was actually scared of writing (what if my work wasn't as good as I wanted it to be?).

Therefore, to avoid the uncomfortable possibility of facing the fact that my writing wasn't perfect, I avoided writing anything at all. This uncomfortable fact was pointed out to me by my girlfriend, who gave me what I consider to be the best advice I have ever received: "Just get it done, even if it isn't perfect!"

After my conversation with my girlfriend, I went back home and examined why I wasn't making progress on my book. This took some introspection, but I finally came to the conclusion that **my pursuit of perfection was leading to procrastination**.

WHY YOU SHOULD GIVE YOURSELF PERMISSION TO BE IMPERFECT

That night, I set asides all my fantasies of writing a perfect book and decide to write *a* book. I reasoned, "How am I going to publish a New York Times bestseller if I never even write the book in the first place?"

I let go of the need for perfection and **gave myself permission to write an imperfect book.** Instead of fantasizing about publishing *THE* best book ever written, I focused on writing the best book that I could write (even if it was imperfect). My motto went from "Seek perfection" to "Done is better than perfect."

Giving myself permission to be imperfect allowed me to get rid of the unconscious block that was stopping me from making progress on my book.

I realize that not everyone is a perfectionist, but if you are then here's a simple method to release yourself from the pressures of perfection:

1 – Examine why you've been putting off the task for as long as you have. Is it because you are expecting too much from yourself?

2 – Accept that seeking perfection is stopping you from making progress. Look for examples from your life when you procrastinated because you were seeking perfection. Go through these examples in detail until you *internalize* and believe on an emotional level (not just a intellectual level) that perfection is the enemy of progress.

3 – Give yourself permission to be imperfect. Accept that you will never achieve perfection, and that "done is better than perfect." **You can always improve what you have once you create it**, but don't let perfectionism stop you from starting or completing a task.

4 – Monitor your internal dialogue. When you find yourself avoiding a task, monitor your self-talk. Are you avoiding it because you are seeking perfection? **Talk back against these perfectionist thoughts** using logical arguments such as "If I try to get it perfect, I'll never get it done. It's better to get it done imperfectly now and perfect it later."

Not everyone procrastinates because of perfectionism, but if you do then it's time to give yourself permission to be imperfect.

Procrastinating on writing your book? Don't focus on writing the perfect book – focus on writing *a* book (you can always try to perfect it once it's written).

Procrastinating on creating the presentation for your company meeting? Don't focus on creating the perfect presentation – focus on creating *a* presentation (you can always make it better once you've created it).

Remember: **Done is better than perfect.**

IN A NUTSHELL

- Seeking perfection can lead to procrastination.

- Monitor your internal dialogue and talk back against perfectionist thoughts.

- Give yourself permission to be imperfect.

- Consciously change your goal from creating perfect work to creating imperfect work.

Realize that you can always try to perfect what you have once you create it.

ACTIONABLE KNOWLEDGE

APPLICATION EERCISE #8

1 – Write down an example from your life when you procrastinated and failed to complete an important task because you were trying to be perfect.

On an art project

2 – Write yourself a note giving yourself permission to be imperfect (e.g., "I allow myself to create an imperfect first version of my presentation. I realize that my first draft won't be perfect, and I'm OK with that because I can always work on making better what I have *after* I complete it.").

Its okay if im imperfect
better imperfect and done

3 – Write down two to three statements you can use to fight back against perfectionist thoughts (e.g., "Done is better than perfect" or "If I try to get it perfect, I will never get it done" or "I'll focus on getting an imperfect version done first and improve it later").

Done is better than perfect

CHAPTER TEN

HOW TO STOP CONVENIENTLY "FORGETTING" TASKS

When I go into work in the morning, there are certain tasks that I just do *not* want to do – because they're too boring, too complicated or too time-consuming.

Let me give you an example: Because I head up the commercial division of an IT firm, I usually spend a lot of time meeting the heads of various companies and discussing how we can partner together to grow our businesses.

While I enjoying meeting new people and striking up new deals, the task that I absolutely *dread* is reading through contracts of 50+ pages. If you've ever had the misfortune of reading through business contracts, you know that they are written in dry and dense and boring language.

At any time I have three to five such contracts sitting on my desk. I absolutely hate reading the contracts (in case I didn't emphasize that already), but it's an important part of my job.

Given that I'm the one striking up these new deals, I need to understand what I'm getting into.

Here's where I have to make a shocking admission: There was a time where I hated reading the contracts so much that I had several of them sitting on my desk for months! I kept telling myself that I would read the contracts "tomorrow" until months had gone by.

HOW TO STOP PROCRASTINATING AND DOUBLE YOUR PRODUCTIVITY

However, one day, seeing the growing pile of contracts on my desk and feeling disgusted with myself for not carrying out this important part of my job, I grabbed a blank sheet of yellow paper (for some reason, I prefer working on yellow paper) and **created a simple "to-do" list for the day.** This to-do list contained action points for the contracts I needed to read.

By the end of that day, I had read through and approved more than half of the contracts (with a couple being sent for revision).

The next day I came in and created a similar to-do list. By the end of the day, I had completed reading all pending contracts!

Over the six months that I have used to-do lists at work, I have dramatically reduced the instances where I procrastinate and more than doubled my productivity!

So, why is creating a to-do list so effective at avoiding procrastination? It's because **having a to-do list makes it very hard to conveniently forget about the unpleasant tasks**. Furthermore, you'll love crossing off a completed task (it gives you a great feeling of accomplishment), and that will get you addicted to getting things done! It will help you create the foundation for an anti-procrastination habit.

If you're looking for an effortless way to stop procrastinating and double your productivity, I encourage you to start making to-do lists.

IN A NUTSHELL

- It's easy to conveniently "forget" about unpleasant tasks.

- Using a to-do list for your top tasks will increase your desire to complete them so that you can cross them off your list at the end of the day.

- As a result of using to-do lists, you will experience an increase in your productivity.

ACTIONABLE KNOWLEDGE

APPLICATION EXERCISE #9

1 – When you wake up in the morning (or as soon as you get to work), grab a pen and paper and write down your top five things that you need to get done during the day.

_____

_____

_____

_____

_____

_____

_____

2 – Next to each item on the list, write down a time when you plan to tackle the task (e.g., "Read contract – 9:30-11 a.m.).

3 – When you complete the appropriate task, cross off the task on your list. This will give you a great sense of accomplishment that will get you addicted to getting things done.

4 – Get into a habit of creating your to-do list for your top five items for the day. This ensures that you will **complete those five items by the end of the day** (instead of "creatively procrastinating" by spending time on less valuable activities)

CHAPTER ELEVEN

PARETO'S PRINCIPLE: HOW TO ELIMINATE DISGUISED PROCRASTINATION

Disguised procrastination is one of the most dangerous forms of procrastination. **Disguised procrastination makes you feel that you're busy being productive when you're actually just busy being busy.**

As a writer, one of the ways I procrastinate is by pretending I am "marketing" my books. Instead of writing my next book (which is the best form of marketing for an author), I engage in disguised procrastination by browsing author groups on LinkedIn, updating my Facebook fan page and reading blogs online. I also spend time messing around with the HTML code on my blog to try to make my website look more attractive.

Disguised procrastination is not limited to authors. Consultants, small business owners, Internet marketers, musicians, entrepreneurs and people in every profession engage in disguised procrastination.

Can you think of a time when you engaged in a form of disguised procrastination?

So, what's the solution?

HOW THE PARETO PRINCIPLE CAN HELP YOU AVOID DISGUISED PROCRASTINATION

The solution comes in the form of the 80/20 principle (also known as the Pareto principle). You've probably heard of the 80/20 rule which says that **80% of your results come from 20% of your activities.** The 80/20 principle was "discovered" in 1987 by an Italian economist named Vilfredo Pareto when Pareto found that 80% of the wealth in his country was owned by 20% of the population.

Since then, Pareto's principle has been extended to almost all areas of life. It has come to be generally accepted that 80% of your results come from only 20% of your activities.

When applied to business, it has been found that for many companies 80% of their revenue comes from the top 20% of their clients (this is true of the company where I currently work).

So, what does Pareto's principle have to do with procrastination?

Everything!

In any given day, you might have hundreds of tasks you would like to complete. However, some of these tasks are extremely important because they contribute to 80% of your success, whereas other tasks are less important.

If you do not classify which tasks are of high importance (the top-20% tasks) and which ones of low importance (the bottom-80% tasks), you might find yourself using up all your time on low-priority tasks.

Since high-importance tasks are also usually the most difficult, many people engage in disguised procrastination by working on low-importance tasks. While this makes them feel that they are being productive, this is nothing more than a form of self-deception.

If you've ever used the excuse that you are "too busy" or "don't have enough time" to complete a task, applying the 80/20 principle will eliminate this excuse.

IDENTIFY YOUR TOP-20% TASKS
Right now, I want you identify the top-20% tasks that contribute 80% of your results.

What are those high-importance tasks that you keep putting off because you are deceiving yourself by working on the low-importance tasks?

Write them down below:

_____

_____

_____

_____

_____

_____

_____

Once you identify your top-20% tasks, make a commitment to focus on those tasks. For the low-importance tasks (the 80% of tasks that contribute only 20% of your results), **focus on delegating or eliminating them from your life.** At the very least, do not engage in these low-importance tasks until you have first completed the top-20% tasks.

IN A NUTSHELL

• Disguised procrastination is very dangerous.

• Identifying and focusing on your top-20% tasks will help you avoid creative forms of disguised procrastination.

• Focus on delegating or eliminating as many bottom-80% tasks as you can so you can free up your time to work on the more important tasks.

ACTIONABLE KNOWLEDGE

APPLICATION EXERCISE #10

1 – Every night before bed, write down a list of the tasks you hope to accomplish the following day. What tasks do you hope to accomplish tomorrow? Write them down below:

_____

_____

_____

_____

_____

_____

2 – Go through the list above and identify each one either as a high-importance task (a top-20% task that contributes to 80% of your success) or a low-importance task.

_____

_____

_____

_____

_____

_____

3 – Identify which tasks you can delegate to others so that you do not have to spend time on them. Delegating low-importance tasks to others is a smart idea because it allows you to focus on those tasks that are most important to you. Write down all those tasks you can delegate to others:

_____

_____

_____

_____

_____

_____

_____

4   Identify what tasks need to be eliminated from your life. Eliminate as many nonessential activities as you can to free up your time. Write down all those tasks that you can eliminate from your life:

_____

_____

_____

_____

_____

_____

_____

5 – Make a commitment to never engage in any low-importance, bottom-80% task until you have completed all your top-20% tasks for the day. This will allow you to avoid the tricky trap of disguised procrastination.

CHAPTER TWELVE

AVOIDING PROCRASTINATION BY ELIMINATING DISTRACTIONS

Distraction is one of the main causes of procrastination.

Have you ever found yourself sitting down at your computer to do some important work, and then, just before you're about to start, decided to quickly check Facebook? Several hours later you're still on Facebook and you realize you've made no progress on your work. Since it's so late and you're feeling tired, you decide to postpone your work till tomorrow.

A RECIPE FOR FAILURE

Trying to work in a distraction-rich environment is a recipe for failure. No matter how much willpower you use to focus on the task at hand, sooner or later you'll end up being distracted by text messages, phone calls from friends or any number of things you'd much rather waste time on.

If you want to start getting things done, you need to create an environment that eliminates any options for procrastination. Here are some tips to help you do just that:

1 – CUT YOURSELF OFF FROM THE INTERNET

The Internet is one of the main productivity killers on the planet. Even though it's a tool that's meant to help you be more productive, it (ironically) leads to "disguised procrastination."

Disguised procrastination is my term for when you're doing things that make you *feel* like you're being productive but which are really time wasters (e.g., watching a cooking tutorial on YouTube or browsing blogs on the Internet when you should be working on your project instead).

If you've ever wondered how much time you're wasting on the Internet, you should download **RescueTime**. RescueTime gives you "detailed reports [that] show which applications and websites you spent time on. Additional reports show how much time you spent in different categories, how productive you were, and whether you achieved your goals." (via RescueTime)

Seeing how much time you're wasting online makes you want to kick yourself, and it makes you more conscious of how much time you're spending online. **Being aware of time-wasting activities is the first step in eliminating**

them. [You can download RescueTime for free here: *www.RescueTime.com*]

I've found that cutting myself off from the Internet is one of the most effective strategies for eliminating procrastination. For example, on days when I don't feel like writing, I head over to my favorite café. The café doesn't have Wi-Fi, so I'm stuck with a laptop without connection to the Internet. My only option to entertain myself in this situation is to start writing. A couple of cappuccinos later, I usually head home having made substantial progress on my book.

There are also many days when I don't feel like going to the gym. I'd much rather stay at home and watch YouTube videos. On those days, through a sheer act of willpower, I disconnect my Internet router from the power supply, thus cutting myself off from the Internet (sometimes I ask my housemate to do this for me). With no more YouTube videos to distract me, I'm able to use my limited willpower to head over the gym.

I realize that heading over to an Internet-free café to work might not be an option for you, but don't worry because there are some great tools available to help you stop wasting time on the Internet:

- **StayFocused** is "a (free) productivity extension for Google Chrome that helps you stay focused on work by restricting the amount of time you can spend on time-wasting websites. Once your allotted time has been used up, the sites you have blocked will be inaccessible for the rest of the day." (via Chrome Web Store) The app is available for free here: *www.bit.ly/free-focus*

- If you use Mozilla Firefox, you can download **LeechBlock**. LeechBlock "is a simple productivity tool designed to block those time-wasting sites that can suck the life out of your working day. All you need to do is specify which sites to block and when to block them." (via Firefox) You can download the Firefox extension for free here: *www.bit.ly/leech-block*

- Another option for cutting yourself off the Internet is **Freedom**. Freedom is an app for Windows and Mac computers that "locks you away from the 'net for up to eight hours at a time. At the end of your time offline, Freedom allows you back on the Internet." (via MacFreedom) You can buy the Freedom app ($10) on *www.MacFreedom.com*

2 – TURN OFF YOUR SMARTPHONE

You're least likely to procrastinate when you have no distractions. Turning off your smartphone ensures elimination of a host of distracting activities: WhatsApp messages, phone calls and texts, Facebook notifications, Angry Birds updates, etc. Once you get rid of possible diversions, it becomes easier to focus on the task at hand.

3 – SHUT YOUR DOOR
Friends and family can be a great excuse for procrastinating!
Shut your door and let your friends and family members
know that you're busy and should not be disturbed except
for emergencies. Place a "Do Not Disturb" sign outside
your door. This eliminates possible distractions and allows
you to focus on your work!

4 – WORK IN THE RIGHT PLACE
Trying to work in your bedroom is generally not a good idea.
Why? Because your mind is conditioned to relax and sleep
when you are in the bedroom. Therefore, **instead of
fighting this association, work in a place that you
normally associate with productive behaviors** (this might
be a library, a café, your office, etc.). If you work in an
environment that you associate with work, you're less likely
to procrastinate.

Given that your environment heavily influences your
productivity, ensure that you work in an environment that is
distraction-free and doesn't give you options to
procrastinate.

IN A NUTSHELL

- Your environment has a big influence on your behavior.

- It's easy to procrastinate in a distraction-rich environment. To get rid of distractions:

    o   Cut yourself off the Internet

    o   Turn off your smartphone

    o   Shut your door

    o   Work in environments that you associate with productive behaviors

ACTIONABLE KNOWLEDGE

APPLICATION EXERCISE #11

1 – Set up RescueTime on your computer (*www.RescueTime.com*). This will send you a weekly email report that shows you how much time you're wasting on the Internet. Once you have the report, **focus on eliminating the time-wasting websites from your life**. "I don't have enough time" should never be an excuse for not getting things done.

2 – When deciding where to work, choose an environment that is associated with work and productivity. List a couple of your favorite places that you associate with productive behaviors (and which have the minimum number of distractions). Examples: your local library, your office, your favorite café, etc.

_____

_____

_____

_____

_____

_____

_____

3 – Download *StayFocused, LeechBlock* or *Freedom* and block out time-wasting websites (e.g., Facebook, MiniClip, eBay). The fewer distractions you have, the less likely you are to procrastinate. Write down a couple of time-wasting websites you should block:

_____

_____

_____

_____

_____

_____

_____

4 – Monitor your procrastination habit. Pay attention to which environments you are most likely to procrastinate in. Write down the environments that seem to encourage you to procrastinate (e.g., "places with Wi-Fi," "my house because there are too many distractions," etc.). To increase your chances of getting things done, avoid these environments in the future:

_____

_____

_____

_____

_____

_____

_____

CHAPTER THIRTEEN

THE "IF-THEN" TECHNIQUE

When I was a university student, I had a terrible habit of procrastinating! If there was something I didn't want to do, I would put it off for as long as I could. For example, I would routinely hand in my assignments after the deadlines (even though that resulted in me automatically receiving a 20% penalty off my final score). As ashamed as I am to admit this, sometimes I wouldn't hand in my assignments at all.

One specific incident I remember very clearly was when I had to renew my status as an international student who needed on-campus housing. This required me to fill out an application form every year and hand it to the Student Housing Office so that they could consider me for on-campus housing (which was substantially cheaper and more convenient than off-campus housing).

One month before the application deadline, I received an email reminding me to fill out the form and hand it in to the housing office immediately. I found filling out the housing application boring and tedious, and I hated waiting in line to submit my application, so I put it off.

Two weeks later, I received another email reminder.
One week later, I received another reminder with the words
"URGENT" in the subject line. All this time, I kept telling
myself that I was going to fill out the housing application
"tomorrow."

However, every night, I found an excuse not to do so: "I'm
too tired today" or "The housing office is too far, I'll go
tomorrow after class" or "It's OK, I still have time to do it
tomorrow." Meanwhile, I continued to waste time watching
countless episodes of *Friends*, *How I Met Your Mother*, *The Big
Bang Theory*, *Vampire Diaries*, *Dexter*...

The final day for turning in the housing application came
and went, and I still hadn't submitted my application! I
reasoned that I could always submit it after the deadline and
that the housing office would find a way to make an
exception for me.

When I did go in to submit my application – a couple of
days after the deadline – I was told that there were no more
rooms available for on-campus housing. All the dorm rooms
had been assigned to those who had applied. I was left
without on-campus housing.

The only option I had left was to look around for off-
campus housing, which was less conveniently located, more
expensive and came with the hassle of having to pack and
unpack my belongings. Simply put, it would have been less

painful in the long run to fill out the student-housing application and hand it in on time.

It was after this incident that I decided to stop being a procrastinator. I read books, listened to audiotapes and watched videos on how to beat procrastination. Using the tools I learned, I was able to get a grip on my procrastination habit. These are the same tools that you're picking up in this book, and I hope that implementing the ideas discussed so far have made a positive difference in your life.

HOW TO TRIPLE YOUR CHANCES OF SUCCESS WITH "IF-THEN" PLANNING

So, is there a tool that could have allowed me to overcome my procrastination (aka "laziness") and fill out the housing application even when I didn't want to do it? Yes, there is, and it's called "if-then planning."

Before I reveal the technique to you, let us look at a relevant experiment. The research study, led by Peter M. Gollwitzer (*www.bit.ly/gollwitzer*), was conducted on people who wanted to exercise regularly.

Some participants were told to plan when and where they would exercise each week. For example, they would plan ahead by saying, "If it's Monday, then I'll go to the gym at 5 p.m. and exercise for an hour."

The other participants were given no such instructions and didn't plan ahead.

So, what were the results of the study?

It turns out that several months later, only 39% of the non-planners were exercising regularly. What about the if-then planning group? **An amazing 91% of the if-then planners were still exercising regularly!**

As the research shows, "if-then planning" is a very powerful technique to help you stick to your personal promises. While simple, it is a great tool for avoiding procrastination.

COMMIT TO SPECIFICS

If-then planning is effective because it gets you to commit to doing a particular task at a particular time and on a particular day.

Instead of saying, "I'll do it tomorrow," say, "If it's 8 p.m. on Saturday, I'll work on my project." This makes it more likely that you will get it done.

By planning what we will do in advance according to a future scenario ("If X happens then I will do Y"), we unconsciously create a mental command that tells us how to act when the said scenario arises.

To increase the effectiveness of the if-then technique, I recommend you **write your "if-then" plan on a piece of**

paper and stick it somewhere where you can see it. Not only will this paper serve as a visual reminder to push you to work on your task, the very act of writing down your "if-then" implementation plan will solidify your commitment to it and thus make it more likely you will follow through.

Given what I know now, if I could go back in time, I would write an "if-then" plan to apply for on-campus housing. On a piece of paper I would write down, "If it's Saturday (date: XX/XX/XXXX), then at 2 p.m. after my Economics class I will go to the library, print out the application form, fill it out and walk over to the Housing Office to submit it." This very clear instruction ensures that I have no room for negotiation as to when I will complete the task. By setting the if-then plan (as opposed to saying, "I will do it tomorrow"), I would have increased my chances of following through on my intention.

Nowadays, I use this technique very often to help me accomplish all manner of things. These are some of the if-then plans I have set for myself:

- "If it's 8 p.m., I will sit down at my desk and work on my book for an hour."

- "If it's 8:30 a.m., I will jump out of bed and drink a glass of water before heading to work."

- "If it's Monday through Friday, I will go to the gym at 1 p.m. and swim for an hour before eating a light lunch."

Ever since I started using if-then plans, my success rate of achieving my goals has gone up. Using if-then planning has helped me develop great habits such as drinking more water, going to sleep earlier and sticking to my budget.

Using if-then planning, I have been able to achieve far more than I thought possible.

What are *your* "if-then" plans?

IN A NUTSHELL

- Vague promises such as "I'll do it later" are ineffective at beating procrastination.

- If you want to stop procrastinating, set an if-then plan. Research shows that if-then planning can help you triple your chances of success.

- Write your if-then plan on a piece of paper and stick it somewhere where it is easily visible.

ACTIONABLE KNOWLEDGE

APPLICATION EXERCISE #12

1 – What task would you like to complete? What habit would you like to create? What goal would you like to accomplish? Write it down below:

_____

_____

_____

_____

_____

_____

_____

2 – Write down an if-then plan to achieve the above goal or task:

_____

_____

_____

_____

_____

_____

3 – Stick your if-then plan somewhere where it will serve as a visual reminder.

CHAPTER FOURTEEN

YOUR ACCOUNTABILITY PARTNER

Do you often break promises you make to yourself?

You tell yourself that you're going to write a letter to your parents, or sort out your taxes or fix that broken kitchen sink, but **with no one to hold you accountable, it's easy to procrastinate** and let these things slip by.

One very simple technique I learned to overcome procrastination was to make myself accountable to someone else. For example, when I was starting off my career as a professional speaker, one of the things I had to do to market myself was to cold-call schools, universities and businesses. I set myself a goal of cold-calling at least ten schools or businesses each day.

The first day I tried cold-calling, I called three organizations. All of them said "no." Feeling crushed, I didn't make another phone call for the rest of the day. Nor the next day.

I knew that cold-calling was not going to be easy, and on a logical level I understood that I would be rejected hundreds of times before I finally got a "yes." However, the rejections upset me so much that I never got around to making more than a couple of phone calls per day. Some days, I would make no phone calls because I did not want to face the rejections.

WHY YOU SHOULD PARTNER UP

Realizing that I would never meet my goal of 10 daily phone calls per day without help, I enlisted my girlfriend as my **accountability partner**. At the end of every night, she would call to ask what progress I had made. Giving her these daily reports held me accountable to her. She's a tough woman and she wouldn't accept my excuses, and that forced me to push through the hurt of the rejections and make the 10 phone calls I had promised I would make everyday.

As I write this book, my girlfriend is applying for her Masters in Finance program. Because the application can be very time-consuming (studying for GMAT examinations, writing essays, seeking reference letters), she has set up a plan on how she will go about completing the application. For this, she has asked me to be her accountability partner. Every night, I check up on her progress.

Some nights, I encourage her. For example, when she was feeling demotivated because she was didn't do as well as she wanted on her GMAT practice test, I encouraged her to keep practicing. My encouragement lifted her spirits and allowed her to continue studying.

On other nights, I am harsh and call her out on her excuses when I catch her procrastinating. It's a delicate balance, and because I know her well, I am able to judge what method to use to help her make progress.

When trying to beat procrastination, you don't have to go at it alone. Whose help can you enlist? Which colleague, friend or family member can serve as your accountability partner?

WHAT TO LOOK FOR IN AN ACCOUNTABILITY PARTNER

When choosing an accountability partner, make sure it's someone who is tough and won't accept excuses. The best accountability partners are those who are brutally honest and are willing to challenge your excuses. At the same time, they are encouraging and will try to lift your spirits when you are feeling demotivated.

Your accountability partner has an important task to do, so let them know that you appreciate their help. Also, let them know what you expect of them. Tell them, "I want you to be harsh and let me know when I am being lazy and making excuses. I give you permission to be tough on me. I also want you to encourage me on the days I am feeling demotivated. I want you to guide me as you see fit."

JOIN A GROUP

Another great way to build accountability is to be part of an organized group that has the same goal as you. For example:

- For alcoholics, groups such as *Alcoholics Anonymous* (*www.aa.org*) keep participants accountable to each other.

- Writers' groups (*www.Writers.Meetup.com*), including online programs such as National Novel Writing Month (*www.nanowrimo.org*), keep writers accountable to their writing goals.

- For people who want to overcome their fear of public speaking, groups such as *Toastmasters* (*www.Toastmasters.org*) teach how to give speeches and offer regular meetings.

A quick search on *Google* and *Meetup* (*www.Meetup.com*) will show you accountability groups within your area.

If you cannot find one, you can always create your own group on *Meetup* (as well as on *Facebook* and *LinkedIn*).

SHARING YOUR GOALS

Another method for holding myself accountable is to post my goals for the day on my Facebook page.

For example, here's one I posted recently:

"Completing the final chapter of my book on anti-procrastination!"

My parents (hi Mum, Dad!) as well as my friends have "liked" the status.

This holds me accountable to them. I know that the next time I meet them, they will most likely ask whether or not I completed my book, and I don't want to have to tell them that I was too lazy.

I have found that when I write and share my goals publicly, I am less likely to procrastinate. This isn't just my opinion – it's also backed up by science. According to research conducted by Gail Matthews at the Dominican University of California (*www.bit.ly/goals-study*), **people who write, share and track their goals are 33% more likely to achieve them than those who don't.**

You don't necessarily have to share your goals on Facebook, but I do encourage you to write them down and share them with at least one person who will hold you accountable.

IN A NUTSHELL

- It's easy to procrastinate if you don't have anyone to hold you accountable.

- Choose an accountability partner who will be both tough and encouraging when you are procrastinating.

- Consider joining *MeetUp* groups in your area that can support you in achieving your goal.

- People who write, share and track their goals are 33% more likely to achieve them than those who don't.

ACTIONABLE KNOWLEDGE

APPLICATION EXERCISE #13

1 – In order to maximize your chances of beating procrastination, it's important to build accountability. Write down the names of at least two individuals who would be willing to serve as your accountability partners. Make sure these are people who can be tough on you and are not afraid to call you out on your excuses:

_____

_____

_____

_____

_____

_____

_____

2 – Approach at least one of these individuals above and share your goal with them. Ask if they would be willing to check up with you periodically to see how you are progressing.

3 – Once you have secured an accountability partner, let them know that you appreciate their help. Also tell them that they have your full permission to be tough on you and that you would appreciate it if they challenged you when you made excuses.

4 – Search for *MeetUp* groups in your area with similar goals to yours. Sign up to attend one of the meet-ups to see if the group is a good fit to motivate you to stay on track with your goals. Write down the name of the meet-up, as well as the date, time and location of the gathering:

_____

_____

_____

_____

_____

_____

_____

CHAPTER FIFTEEN

PRE-COMMITMENT DEVICES: WHY YOU SHOULD BURN YOUR SHIPS

I've found pre-commitment devices to be another great tool in my anti-procrastination arsenal.

What is pre-commitment?

The term pre-commitment was coined by Nobel Prize winner Thomas Schelling. Schelling is the founder of Egonomics, which is a self-management system:

> "At the core of Egonomics is the idea that within each person exists two selves: **the future self and the present (or past) self, constantly at odds, leading to a sort of cognitive dissonance between the two.** Both selves exist within us and are equally valid, but aren't always active at the same time. It's a natural and ongoing conflict between immediate desire and long-term goals." – via Egonomicslab (*www.egonomicslab.com*)

Given that there is a conflict between our present-self and our future-self (our current desires and our long-term goals), *Freakonomics* authors Stephen Dubner and Steven Levitt define pre-commitment as "a means with which to lock yourself into a course of action that you might not otherwise choose but that produces a desired result."

BURN YOUR SHIPS

An example of pre-commitment is when Spanish conquistador Hernando Cortez burned his ships. In 1519, Cortez and his small army of 500 men sailed across the Atlantic Ocean and landed in what is now Mexico. Cortez's aim was to conquer the Aztecs and claim their wealth, so **he used an extreme form of pre-commitment: He burned his ships!** This left him and his troops with no choice but to win against the Aztecs. By cutting off any means of escape, he had pre-committed himself to win!

Here are some less extreme examples of pre-commitment that I use in my life to avoid procrastination:

- Paying for my gym membership for several months so that I will have no choice but to work out because I don't want to waste my money.

- Agreeing to meet my friend at the gym, hence ensuring that I won't give into the temptation of watching YouTube videos instead.

- Not keeping any junk food at home so that I won't binge eat at night.

- Going shopping with a limited amount of cash (and no credit cards) so that I won't overspend.

- Using the *StayFocused* app to cut myself off time-wasting websites so that I can focus on my writing instead.

- Making a deal with my best friend that if I do not complete my book by the end of the month, I will give him $500.

As another example, economists Dean Karlan and John Romalis used a pre-commitment device to lose weight. Here's their story:

> "When two tubby graduate economics students at the Massachusetts Institute of Technology decided to lose some weight, they employed the profit motive to help them succeed. **Dean Karlan promised to pay John Romalis $10,000 if he did not lose 38lb (17kg) by an agreed date.** Mr. Romalis made a similar pledge. If both failed, the one who failed by least would get $5,000. Happily, both succeeded in shedding pounds not dollars, and the initial deal was replaced with a "maintenance contract" which allowed either economist to show up unannounced to check the weight of the other and collect $5,000

for each pound over an agreed weight." – via
Economist (*www.bit.ly/economist-study*)

The key to success of this strategy was that both economists
knew that if they failed to lose weight, they *would* lose the
money. It's important that **the threat of loss must be real.**
If you make a bet with a friend who you know is going to
return your money should you fail to meet your agreed
milestone, you won't have the motivation necessary to stick
to your goal.

After his successful experiment with pre-commitment
devices, Karlan went on to create Stickk.com, which is a
fantastic tool for creating a pre-commitment device. You
simply go to the website, sign up, set a goal you want to
achieve, set the stakes (usually money) and appoint a referee
who will decide whether or not you've reached your goal.
Failure to reach your goal results in you losing whatever was
at stake. Usually the fear of losing a substantial amount of
money is enough to drive those who sign up to achieve their
goals.

As we've seen, pre-commitment devices can be a powerful
tool to help you beat procrastination. What goal do you want
to accomplish? What pre-commitment device can you use to
help you achieve it?

IN A NUTSHELL

- Since there is a conflict between our present-self and our future-self (our current desires and our long-terms goals), using a pre-commitment device can be an effective way to lock yourself into a specified course of action.

- If you want to be successful, burn your ships.

ACTIONABLE KNOWLEDGE

APPLICATION EXERCISE #14

1 – Write down your pre-commitment to lock yourself into your desired course of action:

_____

_____

_____

_____

_____

_____

_____

2 – Sign up on Stickk.com, create your goal, set the stakes and appoint a referee. Realize that if you do not achieve the milestone you've committed yourself to, you'll lose whatever is at stake.

CHAPTER SIXTEEN

USING THE POMODORO TECHNIQUE TO TRIPLE YOUR PRODUCTIVITY

My final and personal favorite technique to stop procrastinating and start getting things done is the Pomodoro technique.

Here's how the Pomodoro technique works: You break whatever task you are working on into 25-minute blocks. Each 25-minute block is called a "Pomodoro", named after the Italian word for tomato.

Why?

Because the founder, "Francesco Cirillo used a kitchen timer shaped like a tomato as his personal timer, and thus the method's name" (via Lifehack).

After each Pomodoro, you take a five-minute break to recharge and refresh yourself. This way, when you get back to working on the next Pomodoro, your focus level stays high because you are refreshed from your break.

1 – Download the free Pomodoro app for your Android phone from Google Play (*www.bit.ly/pomodoro-android*). If you use an iPhone, you can download the paid Pomodoro app for $1.99 from the iTunes store (*www.bit.ly/pomodoro-itunes*).

2 – If you do not own a smartphone, then don't worry because downloading the Pomodoro app is not necessary (although it is useful). Instead, you can use any countdown timer.

3 – Set aside **25 minutes of uninterrupted time**. Make sure you are in a private environment where there are no distractions. It is essential that you work in a distraction-free environment so that you can give your undivided attention to the task at hand.

4 – Use the Pomodoro app or a countdown timer to monitor how much time you have till the end of the sessions. Once the 25 minutes are up, **take a five-minute break** to get refreshed.

5 – At the end of your short break, start your next Pomodoro. Repeat this process as long as necessary.

The reason I like using the Pomodoro app for my Android phone is because the app automatically tracks how many Pomodoros I complete each day and each week. This way I can monitor my daily progress and see how much work I am getting done.

Usually, I try to match or beat the number of Pomodoros I completed the previous day. The Pomodoro app for Android also has different "levels" of expertise that you can unlock, which turns the process of working into a fun game.

WHY THE POMODORO TECHNIQUE IS SO EFFECTIVE

The Pomodoro technique is my favorite productivity technique. Using the Pomodoro technique, I have more than tripled my productivity. The reason it works so well is because it requires that you give your **undivided attention** to the task at hand (ensuring that you won't get distracted and procrastinate).

Secondly, each Pomodoro is very short (only 25 minutes), meaning that it's relatively easy to find the time to complete at least one Pomodoro each night (no more excuses of "I don't have the time").

Furthermore, the short breaks between each Pomodoro keep you recharged, which allows you to work longer as well as more efficiently.

Finally, keeping track of the number of Pomodoros you complete each day adds an element of competition as you try to beat your "previous score" for the number of Pomodoros completed.

If you've never used the Pomodoro technique, I highly recommend you try it. Choose an activity you've been procrastinating on for some time and commit to working on it for just 25 minutes.

What you'll find is that Pomodoros can be quite addictive and you'll end up working longer and achieving more than you had thought possible.

IN A NUTSHELL

- The Pomodoro technique is a great productivity and anti-procrastination technique.

- The Pomodoro technique requires you to give undivided attention to the task at hand, which increases your productivity.

- It only requires 25 minutes of focused attention, which gets rid of the excuse that you don't have enough time.

ACTIONABLE KNOWLEDGE

APPLICATION EXERCISE #15

1 – Choose a task that you would like to work on. Write it down below:

_____

_____

_____

_____

_____

_____

_____

2 – Download the Pomodoro app on your smartphone from the Google Play store or from iTunes. Alternatively, you can use a countdown timer to keep track of the length of each Pomodoro.

3 – Set aside 25 minutes of uninterrupted time when you can work on your task. Find a quiet, distraction-free environment where you can work without being disturbed for 25 minutes.

4 – Set a goal for how many Pomodoros you would like to complete during the day. Write down your goal below:

_____

_____

_____

_____

_____

_____

_____

5 – Work on your chosen task for 25 minutes.

6 – Take a five-minute break after each Pomodoro. Repeat as many times as necessary.

CHAPTER SEVENTEEN

WRAP UP

We've covered a lot of anti-procrastination tools in this short book, and I hope that you have picked up a couple of techniques to apply to your life. You don't have to apply all these techniques, but experiment with a few of these so that you can stop procrastinating and start getting things done:

1 – Use the **solar-flaring technique** to break a task into a ridiculously small first step and then focus on working on only that first step. This reduces the dread associated with the task.

2 – Use the **five-minute technique** to eliminate the perceived pain associated with a task (as well as the excuse that you don't have any time). Commit yourself to working on your task for <u>just</u> five minutes.

3 – **Focus on getting started**: Research reveals that once people get started on a task, they have a tendency to want to complete it.

4 – Apply the **Lego-block technique** to break large and complex tasks into their smallest subcomponents ("blocks"). Schedule time to work on each block separately.

5 – **Monitor your inner dialogue** when you find yourself procrastinating. Replace procrastinator talk with productivity talk. Take immediate action to reinforce your productivity talk.

6 – Use the words **"Will I"** instead of "I will" to increase intrinsic motivation.

7 – Utilize the **Seinfeld calendar** to hold yourself accountable for those days when you do procrastinate. It's easy to procrastinate when you don't monitor how frequently you've been procrastinating.

8 – **Attach the completion of a task to a reward** to motivate yourself to complete it.

9 – Experiment with new and creative ways to make boring tasks fun: Consider changing the environment, adding music to the mix or adding a social element to the task.

10 – **Stop seeking perfection** because it can lead to procrastination.

11 – **Give yourself permission to be imperfect:** Monitor your internal dialogue and talk back against perfectionist thoughts.

12 – **Create a to-do list** of your top tasks for the day. This stops you from conveniently forgetting about them and increases your desire to complete them.

13 – **Identify your top-20% tasks** that contribute to 80% of your results. Avoid "disguised procrastination" by focusing most of your energy on these tasks.

14 – **Delegate or eliminate** as many bottom-80% tasks as you can so you can free up your time to work on the more important tasks.

15 – **Get rid of distractions** in your environment: Cut yourself off from the Internet, turn off your smartphone and shut your door when working. The fewer distractions there are, the less likely you are to procrastinate.

16 – Work in environments that you associate with productive behaviors.

17 – **Set an if-then plan** for when you will start working on a task. Research shows that if-then planning can triple your chances of success.

18 – Write your if-then plan on a piece of paper and stick it somewhere where it is always visible to you.

19 – **Choose an accountability partner** who can be both tough and encouraging. It's easy to procrastinate if you don't have anyone to hold you accountable.

20 – Consider joining *MeetUp* groups in your area that can support you in achieving your goal.

21 – **Write, share and track your goals**: People who write, share and track their goals are 33% more likely to achieve them than those who don't.

22 – **Burn your ships:** Use a pre-commitment device to lock yourself into a specified course of action.

23 – Utilize the **Pomodoro technique** to boost your productivity. Work in a distraction-free environment and give your undivided attention to the task at hand.

QUESTIONS OR COMMENTS?

I'd love to hear your thoughts.

Email me at: akash.speaker@gmail.com

INTERESTED IN HAVING ME SPEAK AT YOUR NEXT EVENT?

I deliver high-impact keynotes and workshops on productivity, time-management, success psychology and effective communication. Check out the full list of my training programs on *www.AkashKaria.com/Keynotes* and reach me on akash.speaker@gmail.com to discuss how we can work together.

GRAB $297 WORTH OF FREE RESOURCES

Want to learn the small but powerful hacks to make you insanely productive? Want to discover the scientifically proven techniques to ignite your influence? Interested in mastering the art of public speaking and charisma? Then head over to *www.AkashKaria.com* to grab your free "10X Success Toolkit" (free MP3s, eBooks and videos designed to unleash your excellence).

Be sure to sign up for the newsletter and join over 11,800 of your peers to receive free, exclusive content that I don't share on my blog.

IF YOU ENJOYED THIS

If you enjoyed this book, then check out Akash's other books:

HOW SUCCESSFUL PEOPLE THINK DIFFERENTLY

"This book is packed with really wonderful mind sets, reframes, and psychology tips, all backed with references and real science. This is like the "best of the best" self help tips. A quick read, but a thanksgiving feast of food for thought."
~ Tim Brennan, #1 Bestselling Author of '1001 Chess Tactics'

Get the book on Amazon:
www.AkashKaria.com/SuccessBook

ANTI NEGATIVITY: HOW TO STOP NEGATIVE THINKING AND LEAD A POSITIVE LIFE

"Akash is a master at taking complex ideas and communicating with simplicity and brilliance. He honors your time by presenting what you need to know right away, and follows up with some excellent examples as reinforcement. If you're looking for some simple and effective ways to stop thinking negatively and a new season of positivity, definitely check out this book."
~ Justin Morgan

Get the book on Amazon:
www.AkashKaria.com/AntiNegativity

PERSUASION PSYCHOLOGY: 26 POWERFUL TECHNIQUES TO PERSUADE ANYONE!

"I'm a huge fan of Akash's writing style and the way he can distill quite a complex subject into concise bite-sized points you can take away and convert into action. The book covers many different aspects of persuasion from the way you look to the words you use."

~ Rob Cubbon, author of "From Freelancer to Entrepreneur"

Get the book on Amazon:
www.AkashKaria.com/Persuasion

HOW TO DELIVER A GREAT TED TALK: PRESENTATION SECRETS OF THE WORLD'S BEST SPEAKERS

"Akash has captured the best ideas, tools, and processes used by some of the best speakers and presenters in the world. He has distilled them in to a step-by-step, easy-to-read guide that will help you discover, develop, and deliver presentations which help you stand out from the crowd…Whether you are a new speaker learning the art of speaking, or a veteran looking for a new perspective, How to Deliver a Great TED Talk is a wise investment that can help take your speaking to a higher level."

~ Michael Davis, Certified World Class Speaking Coach

Get the book on Amazon:
www.AkashKaria.com/TEDTalkBook

ABOUT THE AUTHOR

Akash Karia is an award winning speaker and peak-productivity coach who has been ranked as one of the Top Ten speakers in Asia Pacific. He is an in-demand international speaker who has spoken to a wide range of audiences including bankers in Hong Kong, students in Tanzania, governmental organizations in Dubai and yoga teachers in Thailand. He currently lives in Tanzania where he works as the Chief Commercial Officer of a multi-million dollar company.

"If you want to learn presentation skills, public speaking or just simply uncover excellence hidden inside of you or your teams, **Akash Karia is the coach to go to.**" ~ *Raju Mandhyan, TV show host, Expat Insights, Philippines*

"Akash Karia is a fine public speaker who knows his subject very well. He has an immense understanding in what it takes for a successful presentation to pull through. **A rare talent who has much in store for you as an individual, and better yet, your organization.**" ~ *Sherilyn Pang, Business Reporter, Capital TV, Malaysia*

Voted as one of the "**10 online entrepreneurs you need to know in 2015**" by *The Expressive Leader*

Featured as one of the "**top 9 online presentations of 2014**" by *AuthorStream.com*

Akash is available for speaking engagements and flies from Tanzania. Contact him for coaching and training through his website: www.AkashKaria.com

CONNECT WITH AKASH

Get your Free Speaking Toolkit on:
www.AkashKaria.com

Check out more awesome books:
www.bit.ly/AkashKaria

Email for speaking-related inquires:
akash@akashkaria.com / akash.speaker@gmail.com

Connect on Facebook:
www.facebook.com/PublicSpeakingCoach

Connect on LinkedIn:
www.LinkedIn.com/In/AkashKaria

2087.1456R00102

Made in the USA
San Bernardino, CA
27 April 2015